THE ART OF LEADING

TRUTH, LOVE, AND EMPATHY IN ACTION

— By —

ROY DOCKERY

The Art of Leading: Truth, Love, and Empathy in Action.
Copyright 2023 by Roy Dockery.

For permission requests, write to the publisher, addressed "Attention: Permissions Coordinator," 205 N. Michigan Avenue, Suite #810, Chicago, IL 60601. 13th & Joan books may be purchased for educational, business or sales promotional use. For information, please email the Sales Department at sales@13thandjoan.com.

Printed in the U. S. A.

First Printing, January 2024

Library of Congress Cataloging-in-Publication Data has been applied for.

ISBN: 978-1-961863-16-3 (Paperback)
ISBN: 978-1-961863-15-6 (eBook)

ENDORSEMENTS

I believe the book is designed for any level of leadership to read and improve their style of leading their team. Desiring to improve your leadership style and have a quick book where you are able to reflect and evaluate is a win win! This book provides that opportunity and enlightens areas that aren't so comfortable in leadership and provides some quick fixes on how to handle it. I highly recommend the book to anyone in a leadership role or academy. **Ronda Doward, Director of Tobacco Prevention**

This book takes years of leadership experience and research and distills it down into simple, actionable concepts. A leader at any stage in their career will benefit from the lessons and self reflection in every chapter.

Bobbi Jamriska, Senior Vice President Product & Strategy

The book truly compliments the YouTube video series Leadership Lab and expands on it. The questions for reflection are likely the best way to engage a reader and almost leave the reader wanting to have a live discussion with the author. Finally, I especially appreciated the language this book was written in. It's personal but also very digestible, relatable and easy to follow the thoughts of the author throughout the chapters, no "big terminology", mile long sentences or foreign terms. It made me feel almost like reading a diary of a seasoned leader, who is pouring it all out on paper. **Aleksandra Carawan, Vendor Services Operations Manager**

The Art of Leading is a refreshing take on building one's leadership style from a foundation of love, empathy, and truth.

The topics were presented in unpretentious language, important terms were defined, and the content was easy to identify with. While the book describes that many of the concepts within are broadly shared among many authors and leaders, some of which are included within an included and recommended reading list, this book focuses on presenting the concepts not in some tired scientific fashion, but with emotional logic to make it personal. The Art of Leading starts with why, and it pulls you into an intimate journey that cherishes authenticity and transparency. I felt both challenged and encouraged to understand and embrace my calling, and am reminded that the good we share with the world shouldn't merely be a consequence of loosely held beliefs, but expressed intentionally as our own demonstrated core principles. **Alyssa Holmes, National Director of Service Operations**

Dedication

I dedicate this book to my wife, Nikeenah Dockery. From the early days of our marriage you trusted me to lead. The patience, support, encouragement, and inspiration that I have drawn from being a husband and father helped establish and affirm the core principles that have allowed me to succeed in leadership. I thank you for seeing something in me well before I could articulate it myself, and walking through this journey with me. The way you love people is contagious, and after all of these years, I am glad to be fully infected.

CONTENTS

DON'T SKIP THE INTRODUCTION

Over the last twenty years, I have come across a variety of books on leadership. Some narrative and descriptive while others were academic and prescriptive. I walked away from every book with something applicable or philosophical to apply, but I have come to realize I was working from a foundation. In the Art of Leading there is a combination of narrative, descriptive, prescriptive and reflective ideas. After the initial draft and some feedback from trusted colleagues, I realized that I needed to be clearer about foundational principles as opposed to just doing the work of leadership.

The first section of this book is the foundation upon which any principle, habit, or behavior is built. Our very being. The old saying is you can lead a horse to water, but you can't make them drink. What we often overlook in that scenario is that there is no question about the horse's identity. Starting out this journey of leadership, I want people to understand some foundational aspects of being a leader that will shape how we do, what we do. The seven elements addressed in section one are bonded together by the essential quality in the first chapter.

This book won't give you ten quick steps to master leadership. There are no life hacks or shortcuts contained within these pages. If you are not looking to be transformed so you can become a more transformative leader, I would suggest gifting this book to a friend. Reading the book and answering the questions will only take a few hours from your life. Applying principles, changing perspective, and internalizing the concepts is a lifelong process. You will see immediate results in several aspects of your life, both personal and professional, but remaining committed will yield new benefits day after day.

In today's fast-paced society, we have become accustomed to immediate satisfaction, rewarding hustle and sacrifice in lieu of balance and patience. We view consistency as stagnation or weakness when it's one of the most essential qualities of leadership. Consistency does not mean being complacent or afraid to initiate change. The best definition for consistent when applied as an adjective is not self-contradictory.

Consistency lies not just in practice, routine, execution, or policy, but in the intrinsic principles we hold as leaders and how that shapes every situation we encounter. When people understand your core principles, they are more confident following your lead because they know your heart. Charisma can attract attention and talent, but principles build strong teams and generationally resilient organizations.

You are a leader. Every person who can influence can lead. Many of the examples in this book will relate to work or organized service, but they can relate to every aspect of life. As spouses, we lead our spouses, as children we lead our parents, as parents we lead our children, and as friends we lead our friends. The principles laid out in this book can be applied to a one-on-one relationship, or the leading of thousands, but the prerequisite is your understanding and acceptance of your role as a leader.

I have divided the book into three sections allowing us to focus on various aspects of the leadership journey starting with self, and working out how our actions affect those who follow us. As we walk through these next chapters, I want every reader to understand a few principles I am applying to this book. First, I don't want this book to be another academic discussion on research that is outdated by the time it's published because our society is evolving daily.

Second, I am going to focus heavily on application because as I write this book on select vacation days, every topic we review is being applied daily in my current role as a Vice President leading a national service organization.

Third, I am going to try to resist the urge to make the book longer because it looks better on a bookshelf and focus on substance that you can digest and apply immediately. My desire is to see leaders excel and for teams to find healthy balance, that lead to healthy families, that foster healthy communities that can inspire a healthier world.

I will endeavor to be as honest and transparent as possible. For those that may encounter this book through various networks or referrals, my podcast and YouTube channel are called The Savage Truth, and that unbridled honesty is a principle I live by.

My request to you as you read through this book is to resist the desire to blow through it quickly. It's not a long read but the journey of intrinsic reflection, challenging behavioral norms, and transforming our mind takes time and intention. So take time to digest the principles, and answer each question before moving on to the next chapter. Each concept builds upon the latter so ground yourself in each chapter to help build out the foundation for transformative leadership.

> *"When leadership manifests itself from personal truth, it breeds a culture of empathy, inclusion, love and accountability."* Roy Dockery

Section 1

YOUR BEING

Being = conscious, mortal existence, life

Love enables truth through empathy

Truth opens the door for transparency

Transparency feeds authenticity

Authenticity validates your calling

CHAPTER 1

THE SIGNIFICANCE OF LOVE IN LEADERSHIP: CULTIVATING RESILIENT SUCCESS

"Love is a choice so it can never be forced and genuine at the same time."
Michael L Simpson

A s a leader, finding balance, peace, and fulfillment in your role is paramount to achieving genuine success. Love is a fundamental element that can empower you to excel in leadership and drive remarkable outcomes that will outlive your physical presence at any organization.

Now, when we talk about love, we're not referring to fleeting emotions like infatuation, fondness, or romantic feelings. Instead, it's a profound form of love akin to the Greek word agape, characterized by a genuine desire for the well-being and prosperity of others. As leaders, we must embrace this unconditional love and yearn for our team members to lead full, balanced, and healthy lives. This requires us to move beyond just concerns regarding their material or financial well-being.

What is the divorce rate in your industry, how much community service do your employees perform, how involved are they in local schools or charitable causes? We can become so focused on looking for signs of burn-out in our employees that we have not learned to see the signs of healthy employees. An employee living a balanced life that takes pleasure in what they do for a living will still have the energy and motivation to serve others when they leave the work.

Our understanding of leadership should be rooted in our love for those who choose to follow us, are assigned to our leadership, are required to follow our guidance, or impacted by our decisions. Demonstrating that we genuinely want the best for their personal and professional development will inevitably influence the way we lead. This type of love will permeate our actions and decisions, creating a positive impact on those around us.

It's important to distinguish between love and mere liking, as the two are distinct. To have my Larry David moment, while I might love people, there's a good chance I won't like most of them #SavageTruth. As an introvert, I draw strength from solitude, where I reflect on my faith, family, and thoughts. My relationship with God, my family, and taking time for reflection refills me with energy.

However, I must admit that engaging with most people can be draining. The public version of self that most people project is a facsimile of who they truly are and as a leader I have a strong desire to know the real you so I can help you develop. Even though people have built defensive layers due to poor leadership in the past, we have to get beyond the facade to the humanity beneath.

Sadly, familiarity leads people to treat those they like favorably and those they dislike poorly, creating toxic environments, inequality, lack of inclusion, and diversity. As leaders, it is imperative to choose love over personal preferences. We must love and support everyone, regardless of whether we agree with them, like them, share their views, or align politically, religiously, or professionally.

Equity has become a popular term, but I truly believe that love is the only true path to equity. Tolerance and inclusion can easily become prisons for those in the outgroup because to be given access without true consideration is a cruel illusion. In my career, I have had the opportunity to be the first in several aspects and in the extreme minority. Some of those opportunities were rewarding and others were unbearable. They gave me a seat but caused noticeable discomfort to others at the table.

If we start from the basis of love, we will build equitable teams by seeking feedback, learning, adapting, and creating a safe space for people to be different without feeling deficient. True diversity is about incorporating different voices into the narrative story of your organization. If someone feels loved, they will absolutely feel heard.

Too often in corporate settings, we become hyper focused on the outcome, and we lose sight of the significance of the individuals we need to achieve those goals. We see this manifest when manipulation, fear, and anxiety become the tools to achieve short-term goals. They often reward leaders for this behavior because they met the objective, but it does irreparable harm to their organization and is a recipe for disaster. The long-term consequences of this behavior are attrition, negativity, stress, burnout, mental fatigue, lost productivity, and ultimately organizational failure.

If you aspire to be an extraordinary leader in the world, start with love. Cultivate genuine care for those who follow you and those you lead. It won't be long before you witness the transformative impact it will have on your leadership style and the overall success of your organization. The hidden benefit of focusing on love is that you can't give something you don't possess. I will illustrate this by saying we can't pull water from an empty well.

Leading with love will require you to fill your personal reservoir with the proper ingredients to sustain empathy in action. Your physical, mental, and spiritual health cannot be ignored or neglected if you are going to follow the principles laid out in this book, so for the sake of your team, love yourself.

One of the most commonly quoted Judeo-Christian scriptures is "Love Your Neighbor." The interesting thing is that quote from Jesus Christ in the 22nd chapter of the book of Matthew actually says, "You shall love your neighbor as yourself." Self-Love is not a selfish disposition, but the foundation from which we are actually able to offer love to others. I will not be prescriptive on how you achieve self-love but want to emphasize the importance of its practice.

PRINCIPLES IN ACTION:

Your employee has a child with special needs and has to attend more appointments and school meetings than your typical employee does. We all recognize patterns so the employee will start to feel as if they are not doing as much as others and try to find ways to equalize the difference. Working late hours, constantly apologizing, making self-deprecating comments about the impact of their absence. Leading with love in this situation would involve not only showing care for your employee but their family.

This can be done by asking for updates about their child, school, specialist, caretakers, family, etc. If you ask during normal check-ins, which should be recurring regular meetings with direct reports, the employee will not feel like it's a burden or excuse every time they need to respond to an emergency or family need. One of the most heartfelt compliments I have ever received as a leader is when an employee told me they felt I cared as much about their family as they did. What I feel they were trying to convey was the fact that they knew I would support them responding to a family emergency as if it was my family.

In another case, I remember shedding tears when the wife of an employee died, and I had never met either of them in person. When I thought of what would be going through my mind on that day as a father and a husband, it was an overwhelming feeling. But that feeling is not what brought tears to my eyes. It was the fact that our employee shared this news while expressing his concern for our customers who would be affected by his absence. On the worst day of his life, he was worried about supporting our customers, because he knew the impact of work. This and many others are examples that taught me there are employees who truly love what they do and they deserve leaders who love them for it.

QUESTIONS FOR REFLECTION:

1. How do you define love in the context of leadership, and how can it contribute to successful leadership?

2. In what ways can leaders demonstrate love for their followers or employees, even if they don't necessarily like them?

3. How can a leader's focus on the outcome and outputs of their work align with their love for their employees, and how can they balance these two perspectives?

4. What are some potential consequences of leading with a focus solely on hitting numbers or achieving outcomes, without considering the well-being and best interests of employees?

CHAPTER 2

CULTIVATING EMPATHY: THE HEART OF INCLUSIVE LEADERSHIP

"Anxiety does not empty tomorrow of its sorrows, but only empties today of its strength." Charles H. Spurgeon

Empathy, the ability to understand and share the feelings of another, is not just a buzzword; it is a critical quality that leaders must nurture to create an inclusive and equitable workplace. While we expect leaders to be driven by numbers, objectives, and outcomes, they must also prioritize considering people's emotions to ensure everyone feels respected and valued.

Being empathetic doesn't imply making every decision solely to avoid hurting someone's feelings. Instead, it means genuinely acknowledging and understanding the impact of decisions on individuals and effectively communicating this consideration. By doing so, leaders can help people accept decisions, even if they may not align with their desires.

However, it is vital to be authentic and sincere when practicing empathy. Offering lip service by pretending to consider others' feelings, when not genuinely doing so, can quickly be detected and lead to a loss of trust in the leader. Honesty and transparency remain paramount, even in empathy.

In service-oriented industries, empathy becomes even more crucial, as the demands of customers can be overwhelming. Leaders must trust their managers, supervisors, agents, support personnel and technicians to carry out tasks while being mindful that each interaction could be pivotal in someone's life. Approaching challenging situations with empathy can significantly alleviate burdens and help individuals cope with adverse circumstances.

One piece of advice that I give to my mentees and employees is to never assume that work is the most important thing on someone's mind today. Being mindful that life does not stop when we clock in and with every minute that passes, there is an opportunity for another issue, illness, tragedy, financial strain, or burden to occur. I can think of very few experiences that are worse than disciplining an employee for an acute work issue like timesheets or paperwork and having them completely break down in front of me. At their wits' end, finally disclosing all the things they have been trying to manage while doing their job.

If you start from a place of empathy, understanding that there may be real tangible issues affecting someone's ability to perform or deliver, you will meet them in a place that allows you to work towards a solution together. There are few things that I find create a greater sense of belonging and loyalty than people who know that on their worst day they can come to work broken and not be expected to pretend that nothing is wrong.

In conclusion, empathy stands as a powerful trait that every leader should embrace. It nurtures a culture of inclusivity and equity, making it easier for people to accept decisions that might negatively affect them.

Genuine, honest, and transparent empathy is a foundation for building trust, and leaders must consistently be prepared to navigate difficult situations with this compassionate approach.

By cultivating empathy, leaders can forge deeper connections with their teams and foster an environment where each individual feels seen, heard, and valued. This leads to a more resilient and thriving workplace.

PRINCIPLES IN ACTION:

Walking a mile in someone's shoes can give you an idea of the journey, but walking beside them and asking them how it's going will give you an even better perspective. I have a fully torn meniscus in my left knee, a partially torn meniscus in my right knee, lower back issues and flat feet. Even if we walked the exact same mile, in the exact same shoes, it would be two unique experiences.

As a service leader, I have always been big about spending time in the field, or in the office with my employees. I had done their job at some point, but I started to learn over the years that people's experiences were unique. I am above average height but remember watching a technician almost twice my size work in the same physically confined space. It is great to get into the details with front-line employees to make sure the tools, products, and technology we provide them actually work.

True empathy requires us to know what someone is feeling, not just being able to copy what they do. To truly cultivate empathy, don't just ask your employees what they do, ask them how they feel about it. Do they think it's beneficial to the customer, a waste of time, or outdated? When a leader can get honest feedback from an individual contributor, it's a sign of a healthy team.

ROY DOCKERY

QUESTIONS FOR REFLECTION:

1. What are some examples of empathetic leadership that you have experienced or witnessed?
2. How can a leader create a workplace culture that values empathy and encourages its practice?
3. How can leaders navigate situations where their decisions may hurt someone's feelings despite their best efforts to be empathetic?
4. How can empathy positively impact organizational performance and employee engagement?

CHAPTER 3

BUILDING TRUST AND RESPECT: THE VITAL ROLE OF HONESTY IN LEADERSHIP

"What a solemn thought, that our love to God will be measured by our everyday intercourse with men and the love it displays; and that our love to God will be found to be a delusion, except as its truth is proved in standing the test of daily life with our fellowmen." Andrew Murray

I n the fragile world of people leadership, your word must hold steadfast, and your integrity must be above reproach. As a leader, it is essential to not only espouse your beliefs and principles but to model them in your actions. Your commitment to doing what you say and consistently demonstrating your core values are paramount to your team. As you walk out your principles, your teams should start to see a consistency that gives your words power.

A hallmark trait that every leader should possess is honesty. Honesty goes beyond mere truth-telling; it encompasses transparency, forthrightness, and openness. As a leader, it is crucial to be honest with your employees about your expectations, initiatives, and feedback. Even in challenging situations, like layoffs or difficult decisions, communicating honestly about the organization's greater good is vital.

Many leaders struggle with the pressure to know all the answers, but you gain greater credibility when you are humble enough to honestly say you don't know and then go learn the information and bring it back to the team. Leadership is not about being the smartest person in the room, but being capable of bringing the best out of those who are smarter than you.

Being truthful extends beyond avoiding malicious lies or false statements; it also means not withholding critical information or context. Your employees rely on your honesty to make informed decisions. By fostering transparency, you build trust with your team, a cornerstone of a strong leader-employee relationship. Many of us have had the experience where it was clear to anyone who was paying attention that the company was doing poorly or the organization was falling behind on a particular initiative or objective.

Poor leaders fail to address the elephant in the room because they don't want to discuss failures candidly, so they resort to motivational speeches, treating their teams like children who need to be protected from the truth. As a father of 4, I can tell you from experience that even your children likely already know what you think you are hiding from them. Being transparent in failure actually makes celebrating the wins more genuine.

Trust forms the bedrock of the bond between leaders and their teams. When your team members trust you, they are more likely to surpass your expectations because they want to see you succeed. Leaders who exhibit honesty and trustworthiness earn the respect and loyalty of their employees.

Conversely, leaders who lack honesty gradually erode trust, causing harm to the leader-team relationship. A lack of honesty results in backstabbing and a negative competitive environment where individual survival is the priority over the broader team's success. Transparency aligned with integrity protects confidentiality as well. When there are details that should not be disclosed due to privacy, security clearance, or confidentiality, people should not expect your transparency to trump your integrity to satisfy their inquiry.

Love and honesty complement each other harmoniously in the realm of leadership. Being honest does not necessitate being abrasive or inconsiderate; it can be combined with compassion and empathy. As a leader, loving your team means genuinely wanting the best for them and having crucial conversations, even when it may be challenging.

Too much of anything can be bad for you. In recent months, I have been spending a lot of time diving into the difference between honest compliments and flattery. Flattery is insincere praise often given with the intention of garnering favor or building loyalty. It is very easy for leaders to fall into the trap of offering flattery to keep employees satisfied or engaged, but too much or insincere praise spoils honest compliments. As a leader, we have to properly weigh the value of praise and compliments so we don't dilute their effectiveness. Praise should come from an honest place.

> *"Flattery corrupts both the receiver and the giver." Edmund Burke*

Leading with love and honesty fosters an environment where team members feel respected, and trusted. This, in turn, leads to improved performance, heightened engagement, and enhanced job satisfaction among your team.

In our fast-paced world, embracing honesty as a core leadership value is indispensable. By consistently upholding your word, demonstrating integrity, and being honest in your interactions, you establish a foundation of trust and respect that empowers you and your team to achieve remarkable success.

PRINCIPLES IN ACTION:

One of the most infuriating statements to hear from a manager is that it's above my paygrade, or I'm just doing what Corporate said. They exacerbate this when leaders are not being honest about decisions or policies they may not fully agree with. Leadership often has to make unpopular or difficult decisions and it's easy to detach ourselves from the system to save face with our team. One common area where I have seen this occur is with annual compensation changes.

Most companies have some form of merit-based compensation tied to performance appraisals, and I have seen scores of leaders struggle with having honest conversations about money. So the easy way out is to just pretend that there are cold corporate policies with no flexibility. In my experience, there has always been some ability for managers to allocate budgeted funds across those who are below, meeting, or exceeding expectations. The challenge is that managers who want to treat everyone as exceptional create a numerical conundrum.

If the company has allocated a 3% increase for every employee, those dollars become your budget for merit increase. If 3% is the standard, then I should expect to receive greater than 3% if I am exceeding expectations, but if everyone is exceeding expectations, then they will get a 3% increase. So in short, if everyone is special, then no one is special.

There is an honest way to discuss compensation percentages and budgets with employees. The truth is for someone to get more than 3%, someone else has to get less than 3%. So when it comes to performance, the question for employees and managers is do you deserve a portion of someone else's increase? Healthy organizations should always have someone developing, exceeding, and maintaining. Then, as new challenges and opportunities arise, there should be promotions that increase responsibility taking top performers to developing leaders or learning experts.

Just being honest about the fact that there is a fixed pool of money that has to be fairly divided across the team helps put it into context. Managers also should not treat the budgeted increase as a consolation, but something they have to honestly manage to reward and retain talent on their team.

QUESTIONS FOR REFLECTION:

1. In what ways can a lack of transparency erode trust between leaders and their employees? How can transparency be improved?
2. How can leaders ensure that they are modeling the behavior and values they expect from their employees?
3. How can leaders rebuild trust with employees who have lost faith in them due to dishonesty or lack of transparency in the past?
4. How can leaders identify and address their own biases or blind spots

when it comes to communicating truthfully with their employees?

CHAPTER 4

EMBRACING VULNERABILITY: THE POWER OF TRANSPARENT LEADERSHIP

"We're most loved for our vulnerabilities and our honesty about them." David White

In this enlightening chapter, we'll explore the profound significance of being transparent about personal weaknesses as a leader. In the last chapter, we talked about being honest regarding business decisions, but we will focus on personal transparency in this chapter.

Whether you lead a corporation, non-profit organization, social movement, or as an entrepreneur, understanding the importance of vulnerability is crucial to becoming an exceptional leader.

In the current leadership landscape, there is a concerning trend of promoting fake exceptionalism. Leadership influencers work 12-hour days, sleep 8 hours a night, exercise 2 hours a day, meditate 2 hours a day, and spend at least 4 hours with family. Yes, that is more than 24 hours in a day because while people lay out these superficial game plans for success, they often leave out the sacrifices and gaps. They gloss over the disconnect from family, lack of time to serve the community, missed birthdays, extracurricular activities and special occasions.

Many leaders shy away from discussing their flaws or weaknesses and resort to using clichéd responses, such as "my weakness is that I work too hard." This behavior is counterproductive and fails to benefit anyone involved. In several conversations with mentees over the years, I have emphasized that every promotion was a sacrifice that cost me something valuable for a period, and in retrospect, not all of those costs were worth it. Being transparent allows people to see that burdens are not impassable but they are present, and they are real. However, if managed properly, they don't have to become permanent or malignant if we are intentional.

As a leader, embracing transparency about your weaknesses is vital. Your team members need someone they can trust, and being open about your vulnerabilities is a powerful way to build that trust. However, individuals may be hesitant to share their flaws with management due to past experiences with mere managers, rather than genuine leaders.

Traditional managers often adopt a punitive approach, attempting to identify weaknesses and eradicating them from their employees. This approach, however, is not conducive to growth because people yearn to be developed in areas where they are weak. They seek a leader who is willing to help them grow in their areas of weakness rather than merely pointing them out. Poor leaders push people to perform better without committing the time to partnership in their development.

A common example; you have a team member who struggles with presenting information to a large group because of a fear of public speaking, so the meeting runs long, or there is a lack of engagement with the audience. Managers remove that responsibility from the struggling employee or jump in to push things along, causing the employee to feel embarrassed and retract. Effective leaders would identify the weakness and work with the employee to build their confidence by giving them smaller tasks and allowing them to build to a larger group presentation.

Our cultural conditioning often encourages us to hide weaknesses and highlight strengths. In the age of social media, we tend to focus solely on our successes and shy away from discussing our struggles. I often hear this referred to as the highlight reel effect. We only look at the victories, but skip over the fumbles, flops, and failures.

True leadership demands authenticity. To foster authenticity within your team, you must create an environment where they feel comfortable bringing their whole selves to work, vulnerabilities and all. We see this with the latest push for inclusion around disabilities, whether it's neurodiversity, visible or invisible disabilities; the workplace has not historically been a safe space to share those differences.

Not every disability is a weakness, but as a person with several autoimmune diseases that have caused joint deterioration I have struggled with weakness in my hands for the last 10 years. When working as a technician, I never mentioned it to my bosses, and I found my own ways to accommodate. When I transitioned into senior leadership I had to be hospitalized after a team outing because my body didn't respond well to the activities or the environment. That's when most of my colleagues learned I have invisible disabilities.

Learning from that experience, I started to share some of those stories with members of my team and I was surprised by the number of people who started to discuss the different methods they used to address their own personal differences. Thus, allowing them not only to get the job done, but to exceed expectations. Medical issues abruptly ended what started as an exceptional military career, so the chapters don't always end well, but the story continues.

Authenticity is a cornerstone of exceptional leadership. When you encourage your team members to show up authentically, you create a space where they can share their weaknesses and insecurities. As a leader, you play a pivotal role in guiding them through these challenges and helping them develop these areas into strengths. Self-awareness is critical in this area as a leader because of the danger of what I call compounding weaknesses.

As a leader, we have our own weaknesses and as we identify those; we have to realize that they limit us in our ability to develop those under our direction in areas where we need development. This is why understanding the strengths and weaknesses within your team is vital, because we should leverage the strengths of others to get the best outcome for the team, even if that development needs to come from someone other than you.

For example, I am not the best at frequently offering praise or compliments. This stems from the fact that I find most flattery to be disingenuous and often an attempt to gain favor or loyalty. I am also motivated by a firm belief that what I do for a living is intrinsically connected to my purpose in life, so since God made me for this work, I feel the credit should go to the creator, and not the creation.

So for me to have an employee who is extrinsically motivated and needs frequent positive feedback would be a compounding weakness. In that scenario, I would create regular reminders for myself to be more vocal about their performance, and I would get them connected with a mentor who is also extrinsically motivated, with more experience in how to navigate bosses with different feedback styles.

It's essential to acknowledge that not every weakness can be transformed into a strength, and that's perfectly acceptable. Some weaknesses are inherent in one's personality and may remain constant. However, this doesn't mean that goals cannot be achieved and progress can't be made, it simply means a different approach may be necessary.

In conclusion, transparency about weaknesses as a leader holds profound importance. It cultivates trust with your team and conveys your dedication to helping them grow in areas of vulnerability. Embracing authenticity is key to becoming an exceptional leader, and it is imperative to create a safe and inclusive environment where team members can bring their complete selves to work, vulnerabilities and insecurities included. By fostering such a culture, you empower your team to thrive and achieve extraordinary success.

PRINCIPLES IN ACTION:

There are a number of examples in this chapter, but I want to highlight a personal vulnerability and how I have tried to manage it over the years. The reason love and honesty are the first principles we review is because they can be strengths and weaknesses. Love without accountability becomes enabling that can be dangerous. Honesty without tact, empathy or maturity can be damaging as well.

One of my vulnerabilities is that I genuinely love people. I have seen the depths and heights of human potential and depravity and the very thin line that lays between the two polarizing outcomes. I am a Pastor by calling so I know that I will personally invest more time and energy into trying to develop the potential of others than what most would consider reasonable.

So I use policies, processes, standards, and written expectations to ensure that I hold everyone to a reasonable minimum standard. When someone fails to meet reasonable standards after attempts to improve their performance, I don't allow my love for people to enable underperformers. When you have a vulnerability, you should be honest about it and put systems and people around you that help you find balance.

QUESTIONS FOR REFLECTION:

1. How have you been conditioned to hide your weaknesses and only highlight your strengths?
2. Do you think that transparency about weaknesses can help develop trust between leaders and their team members? Why or why not?
3. How can leaders create a safe space for team members to share their weaknesses and insecurities?
4. How can leaders effectively develop team members in areas where they may have weaknesses?

CHAPTER 5

THE POWER OF AUTHENTIC LEADERSHIP: UNLEASHING FULL POTENTIAL

"I consider my ability to arouse enthusiasm among my people, the greatest asset I possess, and the way to develop the best that is in a person is by appreciation and encouragement."
Charles Schwab

As a leader juggling various roles, people often wonder how I manage to accomplish so much being a business executive, artist, entrepreneur, pastor, mentor, community volunteer, consultant, film producer, Podcaster, YouTuber, author, husband, and father to four children. After much introspection, external feedback, and asking my wife, the resounding answer that emerges is authenticity.

Authenticity means being true to yourself, wholeheartedly and unapologetically. When we consistently show up as our genuine selves in every situation, we avoid what I like to call "hysteresis losses." The technical definition of hysteresis loss is the energy wasted in the form of heat when dealing with magnetization saturation and now we are putting ET2 Dockery (Navy Nuke) away so we can get back to discussing leadership.

For our discussion, I will define it as the losses that occur when we shift forms, similar to the transformation of a liquid into a solid or gas. This principle applies when we are not authentic and shift between different versions of ourselves, causing a loss of efficiency, energy and effectiveness in these transitions.

A classic illustration of this comes from the 1993 film Mrs. Doubtfire directed by Chris Columbus and starring Robin Williams and Sally Field. There is one scene when Daniel Hillard, Robin Williams' character, books two meetings at the same time, at the same restaurant. If you are unfamiliar with the plot, this is not simply a time management issue since Daniel Hillard had been serving his recently separated wife and children disguised as an elderly British nanny named Mrs. Doubtfire. In this scene, you see Daniel transform into Mrs. Doubtfire and bounce between two dinner tables and two different social situations until the exhaustion leads him to slip and sit at the wrong table dressed as the wrong person. This roughly 15-minute scene ends with these dual identities being exposed and showing that when we have a divided existence the two narratives will collide at some point along the way.

As humans, we are not hard-wired for multitasking. We effectively focus on one task at a time. Transitioning between tasks already poses challenges, and navigating between various versions of ourselves adds to the complexity. Authenticity entails embracing our true selves without neglecting our culture, principles, beliefs or fundamentally altering who we are because of external forces. It is not about code-switching or adjusting ourselves to accommodate different people in our lives.

For those that may be unfamiliar with the term, code switching is the way in which a member of an underrepresented group adjusts their language, syntax, grammar, behavior or appearance to fit into a dominant culture. I believe that the greatest way to show love is in the way that we serve and sacrifice for others, so I'm not advocating that we walk around wishing the world to bend to our desires. Being authentic does not mean being stubborn, fixed, intolerant, or exclusionary. When you truly love and respect the authentic version of yourself, you grow to have a greater appreciation for the unique authenticity of others.

When we leave parts of ourselves behind, we operate at less than our optimal ability. By suppressing certain aspects of our skills, gifts, experience and weaknesses, we hinder our potential. This is why authenticity holds such immense importance in leadership. When we lead with authenticity, we inspire and empower others to do the same.

In my experience as a leader, I have discovered that when we bring our entire selves to work; we achieve remarkable results. Beyond my professional endeavors, I possess skills in sound engineering, creative writing, photography, video editing, public speaking, singing, event planning, community outreach, justice advocacy, and interior design. Embracing authenticity means bringing all of these passions and talents to the table, enriching the work environment, and unlocking greater potential.

One window into our authentic selves that cracked open during the pandemic was video calls giving us a glimpse into the homes of those we worked with. Over the last three years, I have watched a lot of workspaces evolve to include more objects that reflect different aspects of our lives and personalities that were previously left at home. I still have the contact photo for my previous boss as the screenshot I snapped during a zoom call of him wearing one of his son's Power Rangers masks. For a CEO and former military officer to show that playful side, was one of the most humanizing things I experienced from a superior in my career, and it earned him the respect of my then 3-year-old son and boosted my stock because I was working with the Red Ranger.

In conclusion, authenticity stands as a foundational pillar of effective leadership. When we embrace our true selves, we eliminate efficiency losses and harness the full extent of our abilities and interests. Moreover, our authenticity serves as an inspiration for others to do the same, leading to a collective unleashing of potential. By operating at our optimal ability, productivity and success naturally follow, benefiting both individuals and the organization as a whole.

PRINCIPLES IN ACTION:

Authenticity is something that I have struggled with for a large portion of my professional career. As an African-American male, I spent most of my life internally and externally trying to fight against stereotypes that are plastered across media and entertainment about Black men. When your interest, style of dress, or hobbies don't fit the majority culture, especially in the business world, there is immense pressure to assimilate in lieu of fighting the discomfort of being authentic.

Add in the complexity that I am also not what most would consider the stereotypical male. I haven't watched sports since I was in high school. I don't follow stock trends. I have never played a full round of golf; I don't drink beer, love practicing martial arts, but don't watch MMA or boxing. Now I can carry on a conversation regarding almost any topic because I am well read and have a cursory knowledge of a lot of things, but faking genuine interest is a taxing activity. Not fitting into the societally prescribed boxes makes most people separate themselves into fragments to fit into some corner of those boxes.

Casual Friday was one of my biggest challenges with regards to authenticity. As a field service leader, my career grew as a remote employee, and I didn't land in an office until I was a Vice President 5 years into my tenure. A lot of people knew of me, but very few people had actually seen me for more than an hour or so for half a decade. Now living in Colorado and working from the office daily, I had to make the decision on how Authentic I would be on casual Friday.

For those that don't follow me on social media, I am a hip-hop artist, avid sneaker collector, and known for my t-shirt and hoodie collection. I decided to start incorporating joggers and sneakers into my Friday workwear. After a few months, I got feedback from my boss at the time that people were saying that my clothing choices were "eclectic" and made some people perceive me as being immature for a VP. To add context, most people wore Broncos jerseys, t-shirts and jeans on casual Friday.

Keep in mind I was 33 years old at the time, so my feedback was, "So being a VP means dressing like a middle-aged white man?" Despite the honest and pithy response, I stopped dressing in my less than authentic style, and it took me a few years to build up the confidence to show up as myself, and in accordance with any written dress codes. Being authentic doesn't mean I don't follow rules, and if the rules are discriminatory, I would fight against those as well. Authenticity is a journey because we have often become so accustomed to assimilating that we continue to learn over time, the versions of ourselves we have been masking. Authenticity requires being comfortable with discomfort, and not shying away from being unique. The only person who has to fully accept the authentic version of you is you, and that is often the biggest challenge.

QUESTIONS FOR REFLECTION:

1. On a scale from 1 to 10 how authentic do you feel you are at work?
2. What are some ways you feel being authentic would create problems for your professional growth?
3. How do you think diversity and inclusivity can impact leadership and organizational success?

4. Think of a current or recent event in which leadership played a significant role. How do you think the leader(s) involved handled the situation, and what could they have done differently?

CHAPTER 6

EMBRACING YOUR CALLING AND INTRAPRENEURSHIP: THE PATH TO PURPOSEFUL LEADERSHIP

"True leadership does not settle for comfort; it seeks out challenges that contribute to a greater purpose and leave a lasting impact." Roy Dockery

As a leader, striving for growth and advancement, and seeking new opportunities, should extend beyond mere career progression. This journey should encompass personal development and driving towards a deeper sense of purpose. The pursuit of promotion should not be a quest for comfort, complacency or cash; rather, it should align with your calling, offering opportunities for meaningful impact and growth.

When seeking promotion or employment experience, the first consideration should be the potential impact you can have in the new role, company, or department, and whether it will foster your personal growth. Please note the intentional use of the word impact in the preceding sentence. I believe we are all called to make an impact that leaves an impression and a lasting imprint on those we encounter. My personal mantra is impact, impress, imprint, which you will find on shirts and merchandise all over my house and on my website. If we look at every day as an opportunity to make an impact, it fundamentally changes the way that we look at the time we are blessed to have here on earth.

True leadership does not settle for comfort; it seeks out challenges that contribute to a greater purpose and leave a lasting impact.

While many discuss work, careers, and financial success, fewer people openly discuss the concept of calling. A calling is an intrinsic desire to achieve something that feels aligned with your true purpose. For some, it may be teaching, preaching, serving the homeless, protecting the community, creating, healing, caring for the elderly, or becoming global missionaries—missions that can be transformed into fulfilling work.

As a leader, it becomes crucial to reflect on your calling and actively pursue it, rather than passively waiting for opportunities. Additionally, consider the realm of intrapreneurship—a path of entrepreneurship within an organization. Entrepreneurs drive innovation and bring new products and services to the market, often navigating the journey alone. Intrapreneurship, on the other hand, allows you to be innovative and develop novel ideas, products, and services within the structure of an organization.

When we look at life as an opportunity to fulfill our calling we become less concerned about the title, the prestige or the income because we are focused on maximizing our impact. One recent example of this playing out in my family is with my 14-year-old daughter. Alena has been a defender of rules and people since she learned how to read around 18 months. My wife and I have been intentional about cultivating that calling as it started to manifest itself, and Alena has wanted to be an attorney since she was 5 years old. So at age 12, my wife found a local Teen Court program where she could volunteer as a defense and prosecuting attorney for juvenile misdemeanor crimes.

As a rising Junior Alena was starting to think of work, and getting her first job but we encouraged her to find a way to get an internship that was in alignment with her calling in lieu of just getting a job to earn a few extra dollars. Leveraging her relationship with the County Courts she presented her resume to a county Judge and offered to intern at no cost over the summer to get real life experience in the courtroom. Now at 14 my daughter is the only juvenile intern in the county and has relationships with local police, the district attorney's office, local attorneys and every district court judge knows her by name. Not to mention the added benefit of making her own schedule and not having to worry about requesting time off for family summer trips because she's not on payroll.

My 12-year-old daughter Alyssa will start her internship in real estate and interior design next week because she has a gift for hospitality and creativity. These internships are in different counties, but we invested in a family structure that allows for that flexibility so we could maximize the opportunities for our children.

By embracing your calling and exploring intrapreneurship, you pave the way to purposeful experience and leadership. Pursuing your true purpose aligns your actions with a higher sense of meaning, bringing fulfillment and a profound impact to your role as a leader. Every person with influence is a leader, and we can't underestimate the impact of a 14-year-old stepping into her calling and working with a generation of judges who often see the worst of our youth. I hope Alena's time in the courthouse not only provides her meaningful experience, but that her very presence gives those around her a sense of hope that the next generation is not doomed. They just need to understand their purpose.

The next step in your career may be a step into unchartered territory that will require a pioneer spirit. Instead of looking around at what others are doing, or at the next step on the hierarchical ladder, you should look within and ask what you possess that can bring value and impact to the organization. My first promotion outside of the military came to fruition after sharing a research project on management with the executive leadership team when I was a Field Service Technician pursuing my MBA. Every role I have had since 2010 was either created by me, or it was created for me, so I was the first person in the seat.

One of the common reasons entrepreneurs fail is because, as the business grows, they have to step out of what inspires them into running a business. You may love to cook, but running a restaurant includes accounting, marketing, customer service and human resource management. You may enjoy planning parties, but event management requires liability insurance, vendor management, conflict resolution, risk mitigation, physical security and customer service. Owning your weaknesses allows you to build teams that complement your strengths, allowing your calling to expand in impact.

In conclusion, as you ascend in life and in leadership, remember to embrace your calling and consider intrapreneurship as a means of achieving a more profound purpose. Seek opportunities that resonate with your intrinsic desires and align with the greater impact you wish to make. By pursuing your calling and fostering intrapreneurship, you unlock the potential for significant innovation and lasting contributions within an organization. A purpose-driven leadership journey not only leads to personal growth but also elevates the entire organization to new heights of success and fulfillment.

PRINCIPLES IN ACTION:

In this chapter, we discussed the importance and power of intrapreneurship. Most job posts that you come across are relating tasks that need completion, projects that need management, or problems that need solving. I can guarantee you that at every company in existence there are problems that need solving with no job posting because the person seeing the problem doesn't speak up. Perspective is important and we don't always have the best perspective from 10,000 feet up on what needs to happen to drive the best results, but we take a shot based on our vantage point.

The world needs more people who are closer to the problem to invest the time in defining it, and suggesting a solution. There are typically three responses to this kind of personal initiative. Less than competent leaders hear the problem, likely don't understand the true business impact and ignore it. Less than honest leaders hear the solution, run it up the chain of command and take credit. Great leaders gain fresh perspective, reward creativity, and elevate the thought leader that brought it to their attention. But even if the odds are 1 in 3, I would say take the shot.

During the first six months working as a field service technician in the healthcare industry, I was working on my master's degree. One of my projects for organizational leadership was to discuss how to build a scalable organization that met employee and business needs. I mentioned it to a colleague in passing and he told me I should share it with our service and operations vice presidents since I based my project on our field service division. I can't recall when I sent the email, but I remember the deadening feeling of there being no reaction or response.

A few months passed by and I got a message from our VP of service to see if I could meet him in NYC. During that meeting he told me that they had reviewed my project, and wanted to move forward with all of the proposed ideas related to restructuring, starting with offering me the new role of Northeast Field Service Manager. I was so surprised I accepted without understanding the implications of going from non-exempt to salary with an annual bonus. It only took me a few weeks to realize I had actually taken a pay cut, but I raised the issue, and my compensation was adjusted. This was my first full-time job as a people leader because in all of my other roles I was a working supervisor or player coach doing the tasks alongside those I was leading. This opportunity helped me step into my calling as a people leader, which has evolved into being a leader of leaders. Don't be afraid to speak up, the worst thing that can happen is nothing, and that's the same result you get from staying quiet.

QUESTIONS FOR REFLECTION:

1. What is your definition of a calling? Do you feel that you are currently pursuing your calling?

2. How do you balance personal growth and career advancement? Do you prioritize one over the other, or do you strive to achieve both?

3. How do you approach intrapreneurship in your organization? Do you actively seek out new opportunities and ideas, or do you wait for them to come to you?

4. Do you believe that having a greater impact is more important than financial benefits and work-life balance when it comes to career growth and advancement? Why or why not?

CHAPTER 7

ACHIEVING WORK-LIFE HARMONY: A HOLISTIC APPROACH TO EMPLOYEE WELL-BEING

*"To do great work a man must be
very idle as well as very industrious."*
Samuel Butler

In our fast-paced modern world, the concept of "work-life balance" is often used but rarely well-defined. As a leader, it is crucial to recognize that work-life balance entails more than merely dividing waking hours between work and personal life. Such an equation proves impractical, particularly when considering the necessity of sufficient sleep and other life commitments.

Balancing these demands requires thoughtful consideration and support from leadership. Harmony is based on individual balance, so trying to apply generic principles for work-life balance is often a fruitless effort. The pursuit of work-life balance is akin to a tug of war, especially for those in non-traditional roles, such as entrepreneurs and artists. These individuals often find themselves working longer hours and remaining constantly available, leaving little time for personal pursuits or self-care.

As leaders, we cannot dismissively suggest that people should merely fill their free time to achieve balance. Instead, we must strive to integrate life and work to create a harmonious coexistence. We have discussed authenticity, and that is essential to harmony because the less fragmented we are as we transition between the different spheres of our lives, the more harmony we can achieve.

To foster work-life harmony, leaders must recognize the value of providing meaning and significance to their employees' work. If employees fail to find purpose and fulfillment in their professional endeavors, true work-life balance will remain elusive. Often, we compartmentalize our minds, believing we cannot fully live while at work, inhibiting our ability to derive enjoyment and form meaningful connections during working hours. The more alignment we can find between our personal principles and the work that we do, the less divided we feel internally.

You will notice that I use the term calling more frequently than career when speaking of my occupation and activities. We explored intrapreneurship and calling in detail in the previous chapter. I personally feel that I have a calling to develop, challenge, and inspire leaders. That perfectly aligns with my profession as a business unit executive, my service as a community Pastor, my engagement as a business consultant and the network of leaders I mentor and influence around the globe.

As leaders, we hold the key to bridging the gap between work and life by exemplifying what it looks like being fully present and authentic. We must actively seek ways to infuse our employees' work with purpose and meaning, while encouraging them to cultivate relationships and connections within the workplace. This does not imply forcing friendships, but rather fostering an environment where employees feel supported and at ease.

One of the most common things that we try to control is how people love us. That may sound like a strange statement, but the version of yourself that you project to others to gain their affection and love when anything less than authentic is an attempt to control how people love us. An example of this is withholding an opinion that you think may be unpopular, pretending to have an interest in a new trend, or omitting key elements of your life that you feel would give people reason to otherize or ostracize you.

This fear of authenticity is rooted in the assumption that our true self will be rejected, so we present a curated version that is more affable for public consumption. Just to be clear, I am not advocating for a lack of privacy or levels of reasonable disclosure. However, pretending to like football so we do not perceive you as less "masculine," or leaving out the fact that you attended church on

Sunday from your description of weekend activities is an intentional projection of a less than authentic version of yourself.

Lastly, self-care plays a pivotal role in achieving work-life harmony, and employees must be encouraged to prioritize their health and happiness. Activities like exercise, mindfulness practices, serving others and hobbies can contribute significantly to their overall well-being, resulting in heightened productivity, motivation, and improved organizational performance.

In conclusion, while work-life harmony may present challenges, it remains an attainable goal. As leaders, we must bridge the gap between work and life, infusing meaning and significance into our employees' work and supporting their self-care efforts. This harmony has to be modeled by leadership because, just as we discovered with love, we can't offer something to someone we fail to possess.

When employees see a leader that can serve their community, care for their family, maintain their health and succeed at their job, it makes work-life harmony a tangible possibility. When modeling balance we empower our team members to achieve work-life harmony, enhance their well-being, and ultimately, contribute to the overall success of our organizations.

PRINCIPLES IN ACTION:

Life is an evolving experience with varying seasons along the journey. In my personal life, I can think of several situations where I had to be intentional about conflicts between personal and professional goals. In 2015 my family and I relocated to Colorado after I was promoted to my first Vice President role. That same year we decided to add a third child to our family which my wife was confident would be our first boy. My son was born in August of 2016, and something about having a son made my absence from home for business travel feel more burdensome.

However, despite having a blossoming professional career, a growing reputation in the Colorado community as a business leader and artist, we moved back to the east coast in 2017. In that season of my life, traveling and being thousands of miles away from the closest family member caused disharmony. I wanted my children to spend time with their cousins, grandparents, church family, aunts, uncles, and great grandparents. I reached a point in my life where being present and engaged with my family was more important than just providing for them materially.

THE ART OF LEADING: TRUTH, LOVE, AND EMPATHY IN ACTION.

I have 10 years before all of my children are out of high school because at the time this book is published I will have a rising junior, 8th grader, and 3rd grader. On the other hand, I expect to have another 35 years to pursue my calling and have the impact that I was created for. All that to say, work-life harmony is not a static state of existence. I believe that all success requires some form of sacrifice because we are not omnipresent and can't be in two places at once.

Working 12-hour days is taking away from your family, it's a sacrifice. Volunteering in your community in lieu of networking to grow your career opportunities is a sacrifice. It all comes down to what type of success will bring you the most harmony in this season. My early career sacrifices garnered successes that fostered a reputation that increased my value, so now I can work less, be present and still earn more. Be honest with yourself about what you are sacrificing and be intentional about not letting anything be neglected for too long causing irreparable damage that you can't correct.

> *"For what shall it profit a man, if he shall gain the whole world, and lose his own soul?" Mark 8:36*

QUESTIONS FOR REFLECTION:

1. How do you define work-life harmony? Has your definition of work-life balance changed after reading this chapter?

2. How can you find meaning and significance in your work, even if it's not your dream job?

3. How do you prioritize your time between work and personal life? Are there any changes you could make to achieve a better balance?

4. How does the economy and work culture in your country affect work-life balance? What changes could be made at a societal level to improve work-life harmony?

Section 2

YOUR DOING

Doing = action, performance, execution

Servant Leaders exemplify accountability

Accountability clarifies delegation

Delegation sets clear expectations

CHAPTER 8

THE HEART OF A SERVANT LEADER: TRANSFORMATIVE IMPACT THROUGH SELFLESS LEADERSHIP

"He simply taught us the blessed truth that there is nothing so divine and heavenly as being the servant and helper of all." Andrew Murray

Section two starts to shift the discussion from who we are and the very essence of our character, to how we lead with our actions. If we can align with the first seven principles of this book, as we look at our style of leadership one thing will become apparent. Starting from a foundation of love, truth and empathy puts you on a well-defined path to servant leadership. Now we will delve into the essence of servant leadership—a profound and transformative approach to leading. As a leader, embodying the heart of a servant not only broadens your understanding but also magnifies the impact of your actions.

Leaders garner followers for a multitude of reasons, but when you lead by example, you are seen as someone who serves others selflessly. A positive impact on people becomes your driving force, with personal gain taking a backseat. To excel as a leader, you must exemplify exceptional qualities across various spheres, be it the workplace, community, social organizations, or family. Servant leadership is not something that comes off with the uniform or our corporate branded attire. Servant leadership becomes an essential part of your entire persona and every area of your life will be positively affected by it.

True service transcends self-interest. Employing the authentic, honest, loving, and serving qualities we've previously discussed allows you to influence people positively. Even seemingly minor gestures, such as holding open doors or aiding someone with a package, can significantly impact individuals. Demonstrating a heart of service humanizes you, strengthening the connection between you and those you lead. As a former member of the U.S. Navy, I have seen and fully understand the value of chain of command and hierarchy. Rank, grade, responsibility, and authority needs to be clearly defined but we should not ascribe a greater sense of value on one person's humanity because of their title.

This can be demonstrated in a simple phrase I have said to my children for as long as I can remember. One observation that I committed to not repeating when my wife and I had children was allowing our children to absolutely demolish a restaurant just because there is a waiter or hostess there to clean up. So in our family, my children know that "just because it's someone's job to clean up, doesn't mean it's your job to mess up." When you eat at a table at home you wouldn't create that quagmire of a mess for your parents to clean up, so why would you do it to another human just because they have a different title?

After raising three children from birth and adopting a fourth I am fully convinced that we are born considerate and start to learn that we can get away with showing less respect or concern for others when we follow the example of leaders in our life. If the CEO is respectful and kind to the custodial staff, it is less likely that behaviors to the contrary would persist for long.

As a leader, you possess a wealth of expertise that can be shared with others to uplift and empower them. Mentoring individuals and aiding in their skill development are invaluable contributions. Speaking about leadership to different organizations, editing videos because you enjoy it, spending time with front line employees—all these acts stem from a core motivation of serving others and identifying ways to make their lives easier.

Cultivating a genuine open-door policy and actively encouraging feedback from your employees is another way to embody servant leadership. By doing so, you gain invaluable insights into how to best serve those under your care. Sometimes, serving your employees means granting them the space to take a day off, offering prayers for them and their families, or simply lending a listening ear to their frustrations. Just allowing people the space to get things off of their chest can help build stronger teams because some problems may not be solved but agreeing that they exist lets the employee know they are not alone.

Truly serving others means taking burdens off their shoulders, empowering them to say no when necessary, and making choices that prioritize their overall well-being. As a servant leader, you must exemplify the heart of a true leader which is a profound concern for the welfare and growth of the people you lead.

In the Art of Leading, embracing the heart of a servant leader creates a transformative impact, cultivating a culture of empathy, compassion, and genuine care within your team and organization. By selflessly putting others' needs ahead of your own and guiding them towards growth and success, you elevate not only your leadership but also the collective achievements of those you lead.

PRINCIPLES IN ACTION:

One thing I love about servant leadership is that it has a cumulative effect that creates an almost unstoppable momentum. There is an intrinsic reward that you feel when serving others with no agenda that compels you to serve more. The more people see others serving, the more they tend to serve in a selfless manner as well. Serving others is contagious, and you can help spread it. I know that is a rough analogy to process after three years of COVID-19, but I think you get my point.

Homelessness is a growing problem in most U.S. cities, and with rising rental prices, the opioid crisis, and a lack of affordable housing you see more people trying to make a living through panhandling. I participate in a number of community outreach programs that serve those experiencing homelessness and there is something interesting I've observed. When at a light with someone panhandling I have noticed that when one person gives, more people at the light tend to do the same.

I think we are naturally wired to serve others but have been conditioned throughout our lives to be more individualistic, competitive and selfish. Anyone who has ever had the privilege of teaching a toddler how to feed themselves has seen how adamant children are about sharing what they have with you. As a leader you have the ability to set the tone for the entire organization. When you are seen holding open the door, helping someone lift a package, taking out the trash, or just simply cleaning up after yourself. I remember speaking with our office administrator and she mentioned how she loved when my team had all day meetings in the conference room. When I asked her why she said we were the only team that cleaned up after themselves and didn't leave a mess for her to deal with. I am a servant leader at home, and at work so you better believe I have relayed the same statement to my managers and directors when leaving a building or conference room.

"Just because it's someone's job to clean up, doesn't mean it's your job to mess up."

QUESTIONS FOR REFLECTION:

1. Why is it important to be a good example as a leader, regardless of whether or not you get a benefit from that impact?
2. What are some basic ways to serve others, regardless of where you are within an organization?
3. Why is it important to be seen serving as a leader? How does it humanize you?
4. In what ways can serving others be difficult or challenging as a leader?

CHAPTER 9

OWNING SUCCESS AND FAILURE: THE HEART OF ACCOUNTABLE LEADERSHIP

"A leader with a humble heart looks out the window to find and applaud the true cause of success and in the mirror to find and accept responsibility for failure."
Ken Blanchard

Leadership is an intricate and demanding role, and in this chapter, we explore the art of giving credit and taking responsibility for your team's achievements and setbacks. As a leader, it is essential to publicly acknowledge and recognize your team's accomplishments while also shouldering responsibility for their failures. As humans we have an innate ability to recognize patterns. So it won't take long for people to realize when leaders celebrate achievements with "us" but discuss failures with "they."

Regardless of the nature of the problem, whether temporary, personnel-related, or resolvable, ultimately, the leader bears the responsibility. For instance, if a team member underperforms due to inadequate training, it is the leader's duty to address the issue. Similarly, if a team member disrupts the team's culture, the leader must take responsibility for addressing the situation. Regardless of when a problem occurs, the leader is responsible for the health and culture of their team whether they are directly involved or not.

Guiding the team towards improvement and owning the consequences of corrective actions, when necessary, is paramount for leaders. Human interactions are complex, and behavioral issues and conflicts will arise. How a leader responds to these challenges defines their effectiveness as a leader—whether good or bad.

When celebrating team successes, leaders must generously credit the team members and acknowledge their contributions. Conversely, when the team falls short of achieving a goal, the leader must willingly accept responsibility for the failure. The team's performance reflects on the leader, and how they handle success or failure defines their leadership caliber. I don't know about you but I have never heard a manager throw an employee under the bus publicly who is underperforming and think that all signs would turn green if the employee was gone. Failing to own the outcomes of your team reduces your team's trust in your support, and undermines validity with other leaders who will start trying to manage your problems for you.

Leaders must never deflect responsibility or lay blame on others for the team's failures. Instead, they should take ownership and use terms like "we" or "I" when discussing the team's performance. Similar to exceptional coaches, who attribute wins to their players but shoulder responsibility for losses, leaders must display accountability and humility in both scenarios.

As a leader, you represent your team, and their successes and failures are intrinsically tied to your leadership. Embrace ownership of your team's outcomes and avoid detachment from failure. Seek recognition not only in favorable times but remain accountable for the team's performance, be it positive or challenging. Great leaders act as a shield for their teams and take the brunt of the force when the organization comes under assault for real or perceived failures. It's our responsibility to provide cover while being intentional about addressing gaps, weaknesses or performance issues. Without effective covering teams are often left running from one emergency to the next while essential functions and tasks are neglected.

In conclusion, giving credit and taking responsibility lie at the core of effective leadership. Leaders who solely seek credit and shirk responsibility exhibit poor leadership traits. Conversely, those who assume ownership of their team's failures while generously crediting the team for their successes exemplify admirable leadership qualities. As a leader, remember that you are the face of your team, and their achievements or setbacks are reflections of you. Tarnishing your team by putting the sole responsibility for failures on their shoulders is akin to punching yourself in the face. By embracing accountability, you foster a culture of trust and respect, enabling your team to thrive and surpass expectations under your guidance.

PRINCIPLES IN ACTION:

Leaders should be umbrellas shielding their teams from the rain. When you are leading a team of individual contributors your goal as a leader should be to allow them to focus on their task and responsibilities with as little distraction as possible. I like using the illustration of rain on an umbrella because water is useful, but can be a nuisance when not directed properly.

As a service executive I see escalations and complaints as that rain. The information may be useful, but I don't need it falling on my employees while they are trying to troubleshoot or complete an installation so the leadership team should provide cover and collect what's valuable for later use. I have dealt with thousands of escalations over the course of my career and I learned that there are issues and problems. Problems can be resolved with intentional and deliberate action. Issues are often complaints based on opinion that we can't resolve immediately.

An example of a problem is "our machine is posting a position failure alarm." This problem can be resolved by taking action to replace the position sensor, align the equipment, or maybe clean the position sensor to improve accuracy. An example of an issue is "your technician took too long to arrive." This issue doesn't reference a service level commitment, or contractual obligation, it just relays the opinion of a customer that we should have been there faster. That could be true, or it could have been physically impossible but if there was no agreed upon response time or service level, it's just an opinion.

As leaders we have to hold our team accountable to commitments, quality standards, service levels, processes, and communicated expectations. We also have to protect them from unrealistic expectations, customer imagination, and hair trigger escalations by internal or external partners. In the effort of providing cover that does not mean we won't address failures, but they will be addressed under the umbrella as the leaders step out and take accountability for the team's shortcomings.

QUESTIONS FOR REFLECTION:

1. What would be your approach to giving credit to your team publicly?

2. How would you take responsibility for your team's failures as a leader?

3. How do you handle interpersonal conflicts and behavioral problems within your team?

4. What can you do as a leader to ensure that your team feels supported and valued, even in moments of failure or difficulty?

CHAPTER 10

EMPOWERING TEAMS: MASTERING DELEGATION VS. DEFERRING IN LEADERSHIP

"The price of greatness is responsibility." Winston Churchill

In this chapter, we delve into a crucial topic that lies at the heart of effective leadership, Delegation vs. Deferring.

Before we explore the nuances, let's establish a shared understanding by defining these terms. Delegation involves entrusting a task or responsibility to another individual, often someone junior to you. In this act of delegation, the appointed delegate is bestowed with your authority to represent you as they undertake the assigned task or responsibility.

In contrast, deferring refers to agreeing to follow someone else's decision without necessarily empowering them with the full authority to resolve a problem. Here lies a critical distinction: delegation empowers and endorses, while deferring lacks a true transfer of authority while putting the task on someone else's shoulder. A common example of this is when a manager tells an employee to find their own coverage for pending vacation requests or risk a rejected approval. Is it not the manager's job to ensure there are adequate resources scheduled on any given day to meet work demands? This puts the employee in the position to go out and try to persuade their colleagues to cover an extra shift, or work overtime when leadership should be managing the workforce.

Taking responsibility for outcomes is a hallmark of strong leadership. Even when delegating tasks, the leader remains ultimately accountable for the results. Thus, if an individual acts on your behalf, you are still responsible for their actions.

A noteworthy aspect of delegation is ensuring alignment between the leader and their team. When team members represent the leader in meetings or other contexts, they must have a deep understanding of the leader's thinking, goals, and objectives. Only then can they effectively represent the leader and ensure that decisions, information, and opinions align with the overall vision.

Effective delegation involves cultivating trust and alignment. The leader must have a profound knowledge of their team members, empowering them to the point where they can be trusted not to misrepresent the leader's views or interests. A cohesive alignment between leader and team helps avoid actions that contradict the overall objectives.

Conversely, some leaders defer instead of taking full responsibility for outcomes. They distance themselves from the results, attributing decisions solely to others, even if they were originally delegated the task or responsibility. This practice is counterproductive, as it undermines the accountability that should permeate from a leader.

Leaders who merely defer instead of genuinely delegating will not fulfill their role effectively. True leadership necessitates owning the outcomes and results. When expectations are not met, good leaders should say, "WE were supposed to have that done," emphasizing the collective responsibility shared with the team.

In conclusion, effective leadership requires a clear understanding of delegation and deferring. Delegation empowers the team to make decisions while maintaining the leader's accountability for outcomes. Leaders should delegate with precision, ensuring that alignment and trust are fostered within the team. Conversely, deferring without proper delegation may lead to missteps and a lack of ownership over results. As successful leaders, you must embrace genuine delegation, empower your team, and uphold accountability for the critical outcomes to drive your organization to new heights of success.

PRINCIPLES IN ACTION:

Poor use of delegation is something I have witnessed a lot in my career so I'm not surprised that most employees don't have a healthy view of delegation either. I see this when I assign someone a task and later find out that they didn't fully understand the task, but were afraid to get clarification. There is a Seinfeld episode for everything, and this reminds me of The Bottle Deposit episode where George Costanza's boss continues to give him direction on a project after entering the bathroom.

In fear of losing his job George avoids asking clarifying questions and deploys several other tactics to get details on this critical project in lieu of being honest. This is a fictional sitcom but I have watched employees, and colleagues do the same at every level of management. People can even be so paranoid that if you try to offer them assistance or clarity they think it's a set up.

Several years ago I inherited a new service manager after an acquisition and organization structure change. In this transition the service manager role would have been redundant but looking at the person's background they had a lot of experience in training so I was looking to potentially convert the role into a training manager for our pharmacy automation division. I have a background in training from my undergrad degree and military experience so I was looking forward to working with them since I had already built the framework for the program.

I assign the project and give a very flexible timeline for completion since we were still transitioning some duties after the org change. The deadline came and went, and there was not much done with the exception of a single presentation, but no further development on the base framework provided. During this time I was actively asking questions, and trying to offer clarification, but they seemed unwilling to admit that they didn't understand the scope of work.

Then I realized we likely had a barrier due to the framework being based on a specific training methodology from 3M so I decided to book a flight to go have a discussion in person and get aligned on the project. When I landed I drove over to our office, greeted the employee and made a few rounds. When I came back they were no longer at their desk, and I soon found out that they resigned moments after I walked in. Judging by the tone of the resignation letter, they thought I was coming in town to terminate them for not completing the project, when

I was coming to help them succeed because ultimately I was still responsible for the outcome.

People can crumble under the pressure of deferred responsibility and feel like walking away is their only choice since they can't seek support. I still think about this situation and try to determine what I could have done better. I could have announced the visit so they were not caught off guard. I could have offered an intervention sooner, or partnered them with my other training team to help get things moving since they understood the 3M framework. I could have shared my intentions on creating the new role so there was no fear of job elimination. However, they could have at least stayed to hear why I came into town, in lieu of jumping to the wrong conclusion and quitting with no notice.

QUESTIONS FOR REFLECTION:

1. Have you ever struggled with delegating tasks to others? How did you overcome this?

2. How do you balance delegating responsibilities while still taking ultimate responsibility for the outcome?

3. How do you handle situations where your delegate makes a decision that you disagree with?

4. Have you seen examples of good delegation and leadership in action? What were the key characteristics that made it effective?

Section 3

TRANSFORMATION AND TRANSITION

Transformation = the state
of being transformed
Transition = movement, passage,
or change from one state,
stage, or subject to another

Transformation keeps the team evolving

Transition keeps the team healthy

Change is the only constant

CHAPTER 11

DEVELOPING AND TERMINATING EMPLOYEES: NURTURING GROWTH FOR SUCCESS

> *"Pain is a part of the price you pay if you're going to lead, and if you're not willing to pay that price, you ought not to lead."* Al Sharpton

A s we near the culmination of our discussion on leadership, let us delve into a critical aspect of leadership—developing and terminating employees. One of the first challenges that new leaders have to overcome is the anxiety and fear of having to separate an employee. Bosses have been vilified in television and movies, and I can't recall a scene where the manager comes across as anything other than robotic, ruthless and heartless.

Everyone fears the unscheduled management visit accompanied by human resources because they expect heads to roll. What we don't often see is that the only way to maintain a healthy team is to remove unhealthy elements from it. If there are parts of a team that can't be transformed it may be time for those members to transition.

As leaders, we occasionally find ourselves faced with the challenging task of handling terminations or separations. However, a proper process must be followed, commencing with efforts to discipline and develop individuals before considering termination.

Unfortunately, this best practice isn't always adhered to, with some companies resorting to Performance Improvement Plans (PIPs) as a mere prerequisite to termination. This approach exemplifies poor leadership.

As leaders, we bear the responsibility of actively developing our employees, whether they are direct reports, indirect reports, or new hires. If we invest in paying them week after week, we must ensure they receive the support necessary for their success. Employee development should not be an afterthought or a mere checkbox—it should be a continual and purposeful process. Leaders should be committed to the effective transformation of their employees through coaching, training and development. If an employee isn't working out we need to be just as intentional about their transition out as we were about their onboarding.

If you realize you've hired the wrong person and are unwilling or unable to invest time in developing them, this reflects a poor decision on your behalf that you need to own and rectify. Separation in this instance creates an opportunity for the employee to find a role where they will have the support needed to be successful. As a leader we should expect that every new employee requires some measure of development, but the effort and time required to take someone from 70-100, is drastically different than taking someone from 20-100.

As leaders sometimes we overestimate that starting score and have to concede that we don't have the time needed to close the gap without having a detrimental impact to the broader team. That's why I admonish my leaders to never give someone a performance plan unless you genuinely intend to develop them; otherwise, it amounts to deceptive leadership, which is simply unacceptable. As a senior leader I am very intentional about making sure development plans have responsibilities on both sides, and I hold the manager accountable to their contribution to the development plan as if it's their own.

Every employee in the organization has the right to be developed and to succeed in their role, and this responsibility rests with the leadership as well. Merely documenting problems with the intention of building a case for termination is not a solution. Instead, the focus should be on supporting and developing the employee until the final decision is made. You may be surprised to find that when expectations are clearly defined, and measures are put in place to objectively track success people will step up to the plate, or step away because they know they don't have a desire to match that level of commitment required.

If you find yourself with an employee who is not performing adequately, yet they believe they are doing fine, it indicates that you've allowed them to fail without intervening, which ultimately reflects on your leadership. It can be difficult to have Crucial Conversations with nice people who are trying their best, and doing enough on most days to add value. As leaders, it is better to make efforts to help them improve and possibly fail in the process than to simply refrain from trying altogether. Don't allow yourself to quietly grow frustrated with an employee's failure to meet expectations when you have never clearly communicated to them where they are falling short and how to potentially improve.

Termination, when necessary, must be conducted with utmost clarity, and employees should be well aware of the reasons behind it. A lack of clarity, leading to confusion, anger and anxiety, reflects poor communication, and follow through from leadership. Emotions during a separation are natural, but it should not be compounded by surprise and uncertainty. When someone steps into a room, physical or virtual and sees a human resource representative and their direct supervisor present they should know that this was the next step in the process and not be completely blindsided.

To use another Seinfeld reference, "the breakup is the most important part of the relationship." When it's time to part ways with an employee don't use this as an opportunity to say all the mean things you wish you would have said but didn't have the courage to. When you are on the other side of the table, don't use it as a time to bash management and the company if you didn't voice any concerns before termination. A separation discussion can include compliments about what an employee did well and a genuine desire for them to find fulfilling employment in their next role. Don't allow someone to leave feeling like a total failure, be specific on the areas of growth while not ignoring their strengths.

I have terminated employees for their inability to meet onsite response times and given them glowing references to companies where they didn't have an on-call responsibility. Many of you have interviewed the candidate who was terminated from their last job and you can still feel the frustration and confusion in their tone because they don't truly understand why they were terminated. Love and empathy should allow us to let a former employee walk away with confidence in their strengths, and clarity on areas they need to work on.

In summary, employee development should be an ongoing commitment, with termination as a last resort. As leaders, our primary focus should always be on nurturing our employees' growth and their potential, rather than merely documenting shortcomings. There will be times when those shortcomings become detrimental to an employee's full success in a role but that creates an opportunity for them to find another role that doesn't depend so heavily on that shortcoming. By embracing this approach, you foster a culture of respect and support within your organization, enabling every individual to thrive and contribute to the overall success of the team. We have to be humble enough as leaders to know that we can't mold every person into a piece that fits our organizational culture, because they may be a perfect fit just the way they are but in a different puzzle.

PRINCIPLES IN ACTION:

The early part of my career was filled with a lot of involuntary separations. I fired my fair share of employees and when I reflect back it largely came down to two primary issues. First we were not hiring the right people for the job, and we put too low of a value on behavior in comparison to technical experience. Working in healthcare technology concern, accountability, responsiveness and excellence became my motto. However, that was birthed from a lot of growing pains and recovering from the wrong decisions.

Every employee that you hire is going to require some form of training and development. What I learned through trial and error for a remote deployed field service organization was that I could train and develop technical skills but we didn't have the organization structure to support extensive behavioral training. Most of our employees worked alone and interacted directly with our customer base. I can't recall a single involuntary termination in my twelve years of leading at my last company that was not related to behavior excluding the few contracts we lost due to the hospital shutting down our systems at end of life.

To help mitigate this issue we shifted our recruitment focus to include behavioral assessments and interview questions that allowed us to better evaluate how they would interact with our customers, in lieu of our equipment. This led to a radical reduction in our involuntary termination rate, and improved retention in some of our most demanding service roles. Looking at behavior and basic skills also improved our diversity. Experience requirements had previously excluded younger candidates and minority groups not heavily represented in certain trades.

This shift to hiring based behavior had to be coupled with a robust technical training program to help drive quality standards. However, we had the infrastructure, facilities, documentation and staff to support more technical training in a centralized fashion. It would have been a monumental shift to provide the same level of behavioral training given the regional and cultural differences that influence behavior across North America.

Development is an investment, and we should try to maximize the return on investment for greatest impact.

QUESTIONS FOR REFLECTION:

1. How do you feel about the idea of giving employees a performance improvement plan?

2. How do you balance the responsibility of developing your employees with the need to maintain a high-performing team?

3. What steps can you take to ensure that employees understand why they are being terminated and what they could have done differently?

4. Have you ever been terminated or fired from a job? How did the process make you feel, and what could your former employer have done differently to make the experience less confusing or anxiety-inducing?

CHAPTER 12

THE VALUE OF TRANSITIONING WELL: ESCALATE, EVACUATE, AND RETAINING RELATIONSHIPS

"Praise is like sunlight to the warm human spirit; we cannot flower and grow without it. And yet while most of us are only too ready to apply to others the cold wind of criticism, we are somehow reluctant to give our fellow the warm sunshine of praise."
Jess Lair

T ransitioning out of a job can be a difficult decision, especially when it involves leaving a toxic work environment. However, leaving a job does not always mean that it is an unhealthy or negative environment. Sometimes it means pursuing career development, personal growth, or stepping into a new field which leadership should support. In fact, the best leaders work themselves out of their job by developing their employees to the point where they step into their shoes. The greatest feeling as a leader is to be able to build an organization and develop the next generation of leaders. The goal should be to step away to watch the organization thrive in your absence, which we will discuss in more detail in Chapter 13.

When employees choose to pursue opportunities outside of the organization, it could mean they are not being developed, there are no immediate promotions available, or they don't feel like they fit in the role or organization/team. Leaders should not feel upset or guilty about employees leaving to pursue a promotion elsewhere, as it is natural for individuals to seek personal growth and that can't always be accomplished in our current role or company.

One thing I often say to my leaders and mentees is that it is our job to develop people, even if that means we have to develop them out. Development can be training, experience, promotions or career defining assignments. But, it should also involve writing letters of recommendation for some of your top performers to take their skills and abilities to another organization so they can move forward in their calling and maximize their impact.

When it comes to a lack of development and team dynamics that make people feel excluded, those are leadership responsibilities. I have not spent much time talking about exiting an organization because of toxic environmental factors because I think great leaders can change the culture. As an individual contributor I would advise anyone who feels they are in an unhealthy environment to escalate and plan to evacuate.

Too often toxicity has settled into upper management so escalations go up the chain and land with the source of a problem in lieu of a person committed to relief. If your escalations seem to fall on deaf ears, start making your plan to transition to another company where the culture is less toxic. No organization is perfect, and when dealing with humans we will always encounter challenges, but we should all have a set of non-negotiable standards and values we expect from our employer and when they are not met, we have to be true to ourselves and exit.

When employees experience a lack of support on their personal development that can lead to transitions. There are a few things I would ask us to reflect on before leaving a company because we don't feel they are invested in our personal growth. First, am I exceeding expectations in my current role? If you are an individual contributor struggling to meet the demands of your job, your manager may be trying to focus on developing you in your current position.

Second, are you investing in your own development? We live in the age of information and there is an abundance of free or relatively low-cost training that anyone could pursue to show they are committed to their own development. I have seen employees upset that their company's don't offer substantial tuition assistance packages while not taking advantage of free training offers in their field of interest through other avenues.

Third, mentors need to be intentionally sought out, they are not just assigned by company hierarchy. One crucial aspect of personal development is having a mentor that can provide you feedback and direction on a variety of life choices. There needs to be a level of trust, commonality, and commitment in the mentoring relationship that may not exist with your direct manager. Finding a mentor should be less like looking for a job, and more like courtship because alignment, intentionality and vulnerability are required for it to be successful.

As you transition, be prepared for changes in your relationships. Your old work friends may still be in your neighborhood or

social circle, but they may not be as close
as they were when you worked together.
Real relationships will retain, but they may
reduce in frequency. Don't be afraid to leave
a company because you're so connected
relationally. If those people are truly your
friends, they will still be there after you
transition. On the other hand, if they're not,
you'll find new ones.

Remember, community is about proximity.
Spending more time in close proximity to
people allows us to build relationships and
see more of their humanity. As you move
on to a new job, don't be afraid to build new
relationships and create a new community.
Your old work friends may still be part of
your life, but they may not be as close as they
once were. Embrace change, be honest, and
have the courage to transition to a new job.

In conclusion, transitioning out of a job can be a positive thing, especially when it involves pursuing personal growth. Good leaders should support their employees' development by doing everything in their power, including vacating their own positions to create opportunities. By doing this, leaders are not only helping their employees grow, but also pushing themselves towards the next challenge and expanding their impact to the next assignment.

PRINCIPLES IN ACTION:

I have had tumultuous and inconsequential resignations in my life. Starting with my first job at a Papa John's where my brother and I both walked out after the shift manager used racially derogatory terms. All of these experiences have taught me that your presence has power and whether we choose to stay, or leave we are always sending a message. To highlight these principles I will discuss a unique situation where I resigned but didn't leave.

It may be news to some of you if you read quickly through previous chapters but I am a Pastor by calling, not occupation. Meaning I shepard members of the Christian community providing direction, development, and discipline as needed. For the last three years I served as a staff Pastor at a local church where we built a number of programs to serve the church body and broader community. In early 2022 I began to pray about the next season of service and landed on three priorities that would require me to make some subtractions.

I knew that I could not maintain the same level of commitment to my duties as a staff Pastor and focus on spiritual development, expanding creativity, and community service, so I resigned. For anyone familiar with church politics, you rarely see someone resign from a position of leadership but retain their membership and stay present to serve and support. To use a business example you rarely see the Vice President of Software Development resign and just go work in software support at the same company.

I believe this principle is even more critical in volunteer and religious organizations because we put so much weight on titles people feel like they can't put them down and remain present. Healthy organizations encourage or even require leadership to transition every few years to mitigate this issue, but you don't often see that in religious organizations. The issue with any long term appointment is that we are assuming the appointee will be static, and that life will not give them a need to step away in a future season.

Transitioning while remaining available is a gift that all leaders should offer when they move on. This allows the new leader to feel supported, in lieu of thrown into the fire without a blueprint of the building. Every significant transition in my career whether internal or external I have always made myself available to provide clarity, history, context, or guidance as needed. Relating back to the first principle of love, if I truly loved the people who worked for me, why would I not do everything in my power to make sure my replacement is successful.

CHAPTER 12 QUESTIONS FOR REFLECTION:

1. Have you ever experienced a bad boss or toxic work environment? How did you handle the situation, and did you provide honest feedback in your exit interview?

2. How do you approach leaving a job or organization? Are you more motivated by the potential for growth and development, or by your relationships with coworkers? How do you balance these factors when making a decision to leave?

3. In what ways can honest feedback from departing employees be valuable to an organization? Have you ever seen a situation where such feedback led to positive change or improvements in the workplace culture?

4. How do you maintain relationships with former coworkers after leaving a job or organization? Have you found that distance or time apart has affected these relationships?

CHAPTER 13

EMBRACING LEADERSHIP EVOLUTION: KNOWING WHEN TO PASS THE TORCH

"Success without a successor is failure."
- John C. Maxwell

Throughout the text, we've navigated through a journey exploring 12 vital topics, delving into the essence of leadership, from love to delegation. While I have shared insights from my own experience, it's important to acknowledge that these ideas are also grounded in the collective wisdom of experts in organizational development and leadership which you will find in the recommended reading list at the end of this chapter.

Now, let us turn our attention to a vital aspect of leadership: recognizing the opportune moment to step down from our roles. Acknowledging the need to pass on the mantle of leadership can be challenging, particularly when we wield benefits, prestige, authority and responsibility. After years of being the person that others depend on for direction and guidance it can become a fixture of your broader identity. However, evaluating our effectiveness as leaders is imperative because everything has its season.

The first aspect to consider is personal exhaustion. It's essential to discern between physical fatigue due to exertion and the draining of energy that comes from what we perceive as fruitless efforts. Are you constantly pushing yourself and your team, yet witnessing minimal progress? If so, it may be time to take a step back, allowing yourself a moment of introspection to reassess your leadership approach. There is a possibility that you have taken the team as far as you can with your talents and you are now experiencing diminishing returns because a new set of skills and abilities are needed to reach the next level.

Secondly, contemplate whether you sense that you've surpassed your prime in a given position. As we live, our perspectives and capabilities naturally evolve along with our family dynamics and priorities. This is not to say that we exclude ourselves because of age, but we need to be mindful that the passion that fuels our leadership comes from how we relate to our work. As we age and our lives change, so do our interests, priorities and passions.

A job that excited you as a young parent may no longer create that spark when you have teenage children dealing with a new generation's set of challenges. The kind of role that ignites your passion when caring for aging parents may be completely different than the field you started your career in. Strategies that proved successful in the past may no longer yield the desired outcomes. If you find it increasingly challenging to keep up with the demands of your role, consider the possibility of gracefully transitioning the leadership reins to a successor.

Ultimately, the decision to step down should be based on a thoughtful evaluation of your abilities and circumstances. Should feelings of burnout or perceived limitations arise, it may signal an opportune time to entrust leadership responsibilities to someone else. Remember, being a good leader encompasses not just what you do, but how you perceive and adapt to changing dynamics.

One of the best ways for leaders to develop their employees is to vacate their seats so that others can fill them. This is important because leaders can block their employees' development, and hinder their growth potential by merely being present.

Organizations can become so dependent on the expertise and experience of an individual that the very organizational structure stifles upward mobility because there is a unicorn in a senior leadership role. If you are the glue holding an amalgam of strange cross functional teams together because of your unique experience, you are likely creating a ceiling for those under you who would otherwise be leading separate functional departments.

I apologize if it's a bit morbid, but I often use the analogy that, if you died today what would the organization do in response. Would they hire a direct replacement, restructure the organization, absorb your team into other functional groups, etc. As a person diagnosed with several chronic illnesses I am frequently reminded of the frailty of life. I lead my team as if tomorrow is not a guarantee, so they have to be empowered daily to trust their intuition and be confident in the decisions they make.

When a leader notices that they have become the upper limit for their team, they should start planning on transition. This is a good situation to have as a leader, because it shows that you have had a positive impact on your team's growth and development. If a team can continue to thrive after a transition in leadership, it shows that you have done your job well.

Embrace this growth-oriented mindset, by performing a candid appraisal of your abilities and the intrinsic reward you feel towards the work. By doing so, you can make the best decision, not only for yourself but also for the continued success of your team.

Great leaders should see succession as the new branch of a growing legacy and not the ending. Over the course of my career I have had the pleasure of promoting dozens of people into leadership, and advanced technical roles. I personally can't think of any greater feeling than being able to recommend my direct report for a promotion in my resignation letter, and watching them succeed in my absence. Leaders create, but we are not the cog that keeps the machine running. As we make an impact, that leaves an impression, with a permanent imprint on those we lead, we should be able to walk away and enjoy the artwork from a distance.

Thank you for joining me on this transformative journey through the Leadership Lab. As you embark on your own leadership odyssey, I extend my heartfelt wishes for success and fulfillment. Embrace the lessons learned and continue to lead with purpose, passion, and unwavering integrity. I wish you all the best and may your leadership legacy inspire others to shine brightly on their own leadership paths.

PRINCIPLES IN ACTION:

Every season has an ending and we have to be mindful as leaders to not overstay our welcome because of comfort, complacency, or fear. My career change in 2022 was the culmination of a 7-year journey that I can't fully capture here, but you can view the YouTube video where I discuss it in more detail on The Savage Truth Network channel, video name: Where is your story leading you? 7 years of small steps leads to huge changes in direction.

I was asked once what would make me leave my job. Without much hesitation I have two points that still hold true for me today. First, if the company does anything that puts my integrity in question. That would include requiring me to communicate false information, or putting me in a position where my reputation for truth is compromised. Second would be failing to provide me the space and opportunity to develop and promote my team.

I never had to deal with a conflict related to the first point through court cases, depositions and scandals. I was always respected and appreciated for being truthful. When it came to the second principle, because of the direction of the company and my personal priorities I hit a ceiling on vertical growth and limited opportunities to add breadth. Due to systems, processes and great leadership I was no longer regularly consulted for escalations and issues, and when the pandemic essentially eliminated my need for travel I felt like I was only effectively contributing about 12-16 hours per week.

So when we had a change in CEO and another org structure shift, when I was asked to help construct the future of service, I removed myself from the equation. My team no longer needed me to achieve the results we were seeing, and I had become the ceiling for their growth. I loved my job and the people that I had the privilege of leading, but I can't love them and limit their growth potential at the same time. Shortly after I documented and articulated this reality I was contacted by an executive headhunter to build out the field service department at a new and exciting startup company.

I don't believe in coincidences. I was prayerful about writing myself out of a job and God gave me peace with my decision. That was followed by an unsolicited job offer that would offer new challenges and a new industry that works with the justice system I had grown more passionate about impacting. It was a tough decision not because of the job, but as I discussed in Chapter 12, it was the relationships. These are people who knew my eating habits better than my family because of how much time we spent on the road together. They were not just my employees, and colleagues they were my friends, but I love them too much to be the limiter on their upward mobility.

In my resignation letter I recommended my director, friend and mentee as my replacement. It was a smooth transition and it has been amazing watching him build his own reputation as a thought leader in the field service industry.

One fallacy that I want to put to bed now is also the idea that seniority and leadership are synonymous. More than 95% of my direct reports over the past 13 years have been older and more tenured than me. They were often at the company, or in the industry longer than me and 5 to 20+ years my senior in age. I can confidently say that the principles in the book work across generations, genders, ethnicities, religions, political preferences, and other demographics we use to divide ourselves.

"Love is the great equalizer and I believe the only true way to achieve

equity, equality and meaningful diversity." Roy Dockery

QUESTIONS FOR REFLECTION:

1. Regarding personal exhaustion, how do you differentiate between ordinary fatigue and burnout, and what strategies can you implement to prevent it from hindering your effectiveness?

2. As a leader, how do you evaluate whether you're still operating at your prime? What signs or indicators help you recognize when it may be necessary to adapt your leadership approach or consider transitioning leadership responsibilities?

3. Consider your leadership legacy. How do you want to be remembered as a leader? What steps can you take now to ensure that your leadership

leaves a positive and lasting impact on your team and organization?

4. As you bid farewell to the Leadership Lab, what are your key takeaways from this transformative journey? How do you plan to apply these insights and lessons to continue evolving as a purpose-driven and impactful leader?

BOOK RECOMMENDATIONS:

1. Activating Your Brain, Steven Halford
2. Bankable Leadership, Tasha Eurich
3. Advice on Dying and Living a Better Life, Dalai Lama
4. Crucial Conversations, Tools for Talking When Stakes Are High, Patterson, Granny, McMillan, Switzler
5. Getting Naked, Patrick Lencioni
6. How to Win Friends and Influence People, Dale Carnegie
7. Humility, Andrew Murray
8. Make Your Bed, Admiral William H. McRaven
9. Making Rain, Andrew Sobel
10. Switch, Chip and Dan Heath
11. The Art of Happiness, Dalai Lama
12. The Art of War, Sun Tzu
13. The Balance Myth, Teresa Taylor
14. The Emotionally Healthy Leader, Peter Scazzero

15. The Five Dysfunctions of a Team, Patrick Lencioni
16. The Power of Focus, Jack Canfield
17. Think and Grow Rich, Napoleon Hill
18. Drive, The Surprising Truth about What Motivates Us, Daniel Pink
19. Hit Refresh, Satya Nadella
20. Leading On Empty, Wayne Cordeiro
21. Nudge, Richard Thaler and Cass Sunstein
22. Positive Leadership, Kim Cameron
23. Sludge, Cass R. Sunstein
24. Subtract Leidy Klotz
25. The Advantage, Patrick Lencioni
26. The Heart of Business, Hubert Joly
27. The One Thing, Gary Keller
28. The Art of Worldly Wisdom, Baltasar Gracian
29. What Clients Really Want, Chantell Glenville
30. Lead Like Jesus, Ken Blanchard

ABOUT THE AUTHOR

Roy A. Dockery

 Roy A. Dockery is a multi-faceted individual whose life journey has been nothing short of remarkable. Born on November 30th, 1982, in Colorado Springs, Colorado, he emerged into a world filled with challenges and adversity. Roy's early life was marked by a family that was constantly in flux, with parents facing the hardships of a troubled marriage and an environment rife with social issues, including crime, drugs, and violence.

Roy's story is one of resilience and determination. Despite the obstacles he faced, he managed to find love during his high school years, even though it was far from a fairy tale romance. The challenges he faced during his early years only served to fuel his determination to succeed. His wife, Keena, played a pivotal role in his journey, supporting and motivating him to pursue higher education and achieve excellence.

Roy's dedication and unwavering commitment to personal growth propelled him to overcome adversity. Despite being faced with health issues and the unexpected end of his military career, he persevered. His journey led him to take on a range of responsibilities, from Field Service Technician to Vice President of a prominent healthcare technology company.

Throughout his adult life, Roy found inspiration in his faith and the love of his family. He considers himself fortunate to be the husband and father of an extraordinary family. His unwavering faith in God and the support of his loved ones have been the driving forces behind his professional success, artistic endeavors, and community service.

Roy is a multifaceted individual whose journey encompasses various roles and accomplishments. He is not only a globally recognized visionary leader and author, but also an artist, movie producer, and juvenile justice advocate. He has earned a reputation as an inspirational leader across North America and beyond.

His extensive background includes a Master of Business Administration, a Bachelor's degree in Business Management,

Information Technology, and Nuclear Engineering Technology. In addition to his professional achievements, Roy is a sought-after public speaker on leadership, emerging technology, culture, diversity and service excellence.

Beyond his written works and speaking engagements, Roy is also involved in community health, juvenile justice, and civil legal aid. He serves as an advisor for research organizations and corporations, providing insights into fields such as field services, Diversity Equity & Inclusion, recruitment, culture, and leadership.

In summary, Roy A. Dockery is a remarkable individual whose life journey, characterized by resilience, faith, and determination, has led him to inspire change and excel in various fields. His impact as a leader, author, speaker, and community activist continues to touch the lives of many, making him a notable figure across North America and beyond. To learn more about Roy A. Dockery and his upcoming projects and speaking engagements, visit his official website at www.roydockery.org.

https://Facebook.com/PastorRoyDockery
https://Instagram.com/PastorRoyDockery
https://LinkedIn.com/in/RoyDockery
Website: https://roydockery.org

Printed in the USA
CPSIA information can be obtained
at www.ICGtesting.com
CBHW072233070124
3212CB00002B/5

9 781961 863163